# Beauty FROM Ashes

HOW MY FAITH HELPED ME RISE FROM THE
DEPTHS OF LIVING WITH CYCLICAL DEPRESSION

## Quan Ruby

First published by Ultimate World Publishing 2025
Copyright © 2025 Quan Ruby

ISBN

Paperback: 978-1-923425-75-0
Ebook: 978-1-923425-76-7

Quan Ruby has asserted her rights under the Copyright, Designs and Patents Act 1988 to be identified as the author of this work. The information in this book is based on the author's experiences and opinions. The publisher specifically disclaims responsibility for any adverse consequences which may result from use of the information contained herein. Permission to use information has been sought by the author. Any breaches will be rectified in further editions of the book.

All rights reserved. No part of this publication may be reproduced, stored in or introduced into a retrieval system, or transmitted in any form, or by any means (electronic, mechanical, photocopying, recording or otherwise) without the prior written permission of the author. Any person who does any unauthorised act in relation to this publication may be liable to criminal prosecution and civil claims for damages. Enquiries should be made through the publisher.

**Cover design:** Ultimate World Publishing
**Layout and typesetting:** Ultimate World Publishing
**Editor:** Vanessa McKay
**Cover Image Copyright:** Maxim Blinkov-Shutterstock.com

Ultimate World Publishing
Diamond Creek,
Victoria Australia 3089
www.writeabook.com.au

# Foreword: Beauty from Ashes

My wife, Helen and I have known Ho Hoe Sing and Quan for over 30 years, initially as our Church Zone Pastors progressing to being good friends.

Quan has an effervescent personality but is subjected to frequent mood swings that last for varying periods of time. The most recent episode before her 'dramatic recovery' lasted for six years and brought her to the doldrums, even harbouring suicidal thoughts.

This book is her testimony of her struggles and the victory she found in the Grace of God. Through a combination of faithfully studying scriptures, reading Christian books by various authors that facilitated a 'renewing of her mind', a faithful husband who stood by her through 'thick and thin', friends who continue to support and not judge her and God's Mercy and Grace, she has since miraculously recovered.

She is now excited about life, grateful for a 'second chance' to live life to its fullest. This book is not merely a recounting of her trials: it provides a beacon of Hope for all who find themselves ensnared in the grip of mental anguish.

Quan offers a candid and courageous narrative revealing the depth of suffering and her transformational journey towards healing.

It testifies of a God who remains faithful even when we are faithless and in His 'kairos' time will bring His purposes in us, to pass for His Glory and our ultimate 'good'.

I would recommend this book, particularly to those who are passing through the 'valley of darkness'…

Helen Dieu n Dieu

# Foreword

During the several years and many trips to Singapore, I had the pleasure of meeting and teaching many outstanding people. Faith Community Baptist Church invited me to equip its ministry staff and key members with the relational skills and insights of shepherding a large congregation with a cell group structure.

At one of our early gatherings with a key group, I met Guat Quan Khor and immediately saw she was an unusually active member of the group. As I continued several visits each year, sometimes with my wife, Karen, we enjoyed learning to enjoy Indian food with Guat Quan and Ho Seng.

Each worked diligently to understand our unique approach to developing healthy individuals, families, and churches. Guat Quan was especially interested in learning about Family Systems and doing Genograms to show her family's history.

As she interviewed her relatives about her family system, facts emerged that were explanatory and distressing. Her book is a history of her intensive and extensive efforts to clarify and heal the traumatic events she had experienced as the memories flooded her thoughts and emotions.

I am very pleased that my training and close friendship have been instrumental in her progressive healing. This is a strong testimony to her spiritual and emotional resilience, which kept her commitment to Christ as foundational to her recovery.

Dr Gary Sweeten

# Contents

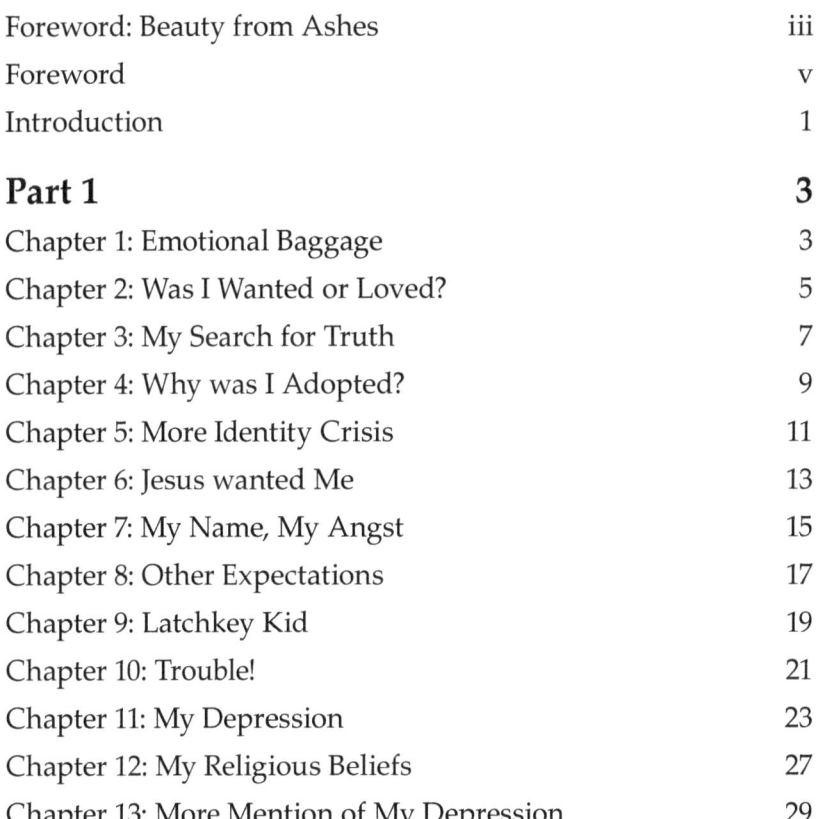

| | |
|---|---|
| Foreword: Beauty from Ashes | iii |
| Foreword | v |
| Introduction | 1 |

## Part 1 — 3

| | |
|---|---|
| Chapter 1: Emotional Baggage | 3 |
| Chapter 2: Was I Wanted or Loved? | 5 |
| Chapter 3: My Search for Truth | 7 |
| Chapter 4: Why was I Adopted? | 9 |
| Chapter 5: More Identity Crisis | 11 |
| Chapter 6: Jesus wanted Me | 13 |
| Chapter 7: My Name, My Angst | 15 |
| Chapter 8: Other Expectations | 17 |
| Chapter 9: Latchkey Kid | 19 |
| Chapter 10: Trouble! | 21 |
| Chapter 11: My Depression | 23 |
| Chapter 12: My Religious Beliefs | 27 |
| Chapter 13: More Mention of My Depression | 29 |

| | |
|---|---|
| Chapter 14: Suicidal Thoughts | 33 |
| Chapter 15: Where was Jesus? | 35 |
| Chapter 16: Conclusion | 45 |

## Part 2: Transformation — 47

| | |
|---|---|
| Chapter 1: A Process | 49 |
| Chapter 2: My Beliefs | 51 |
| Chapter 3: My Struggle with the Holy Spirit (part 1) | 55 |
| Chapter 4: The Work of Holy Spirit, My Struggle (part 2) | 61 |
| Chapter 5: Growing My Spirit Man | 63 |
| Chapter 6: My Soul | 69 |
| Chapter 7: My body | 75 |
| Chapter 8: My Role | 77 |
| Chapter 9: Jesus is a Safe Person | 87 |
| Chapter 10: Forgiving God | 89 |
| Chapter 11: Limbic Lag | 91 |
| Chapter 12: Progressive Sanctification | 95 |
| Chapter 13: Confession of Sins | 99 |
| Chapter 14: Repentance | 103 |
| Chapter 15: Blessing My Enemies | 107 |
| Chapter 16: My Reflection | 111 |

## Part 3: My Future: Jesus Redeems — 113

| | |
|---|---|
| Chapter 1: My Name | 115 |
| Chapter 2: More Experiences | 117 |
| Chapter 3: Return of My Losses | 121 |

## Part 4: Conclusion — 137

| | |
|---|---|
| About The Author | 143 |

# Introduction

"*Many years ago, after years of ministry, I was driven to the conclusion that the 2 major causes of most emotional problems among Evangelical Christians are these:*

*1. The failure to understand, receive, and live out God's unconditional grace and forgiveness.*

*2. The failure to give out that unconditional love, forgiveness and grace to other people.*" **David Seamands.**

I can identify with Seamands' statement. In my book 'Beauty from Ashes,' I tell how in my 46 years journey with my Saviour and Lord Christ Jesus, He transformed me, progressively until from an ugly caterpillar I emerged as a beautiful butterfly, free to fly wherever I wish to go. In His long suffering with me, my Lord Christ gently but firmly, nudged me to get out of my cocoon.

Hallelujah! All praises to my Savior and Lord Christ Jesus!

My book is divided into 3 parts

Part 1: My Past: Emotional Baggage

Part 2: My Present: Transformation

Part 3: My Future: Jesus Redeems.

Each part has a photograph of myself and a picture of my Nagomi art to depict the different parts of my relationship with Jesus.

As the adage says: A picture speaks a thousand words.

# PART 1

## CHAPTER 1

# Emotional Baggage

*My Complex Family System: To whom do I belong?*

I was given up for adoption immediately upon my birth to a lady who was a sister to my biological mother. These two ladies were separately adopted by a lady, who owned a brothel.

## My Foster Mother: The Chinese Culture.

My foster mother was the third wife of Mr Khor.

In 1900s, it was common practice for Chinese men to have more than one wife. The wealthier the man, the more wives he had. It was also understood that the other wives were to submit to the man's first wife.

My foster mother had adopted me after the death of Mr. Khor.

In the Chinese culture, if a child was not adopted by the man of the house, the child was not considered as a member of his household. I experienced the truth of that fact when I was not given a share of the Khor family's inheritance, upon the death of Mr. Khor's first wife. That event was a declaration that I was not recognised as a member of the Khor household.

# Chapter 2

# Was I Wanted or Loved?

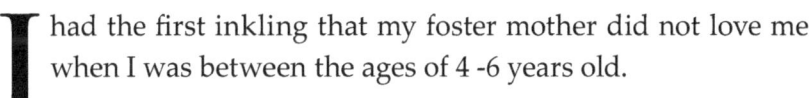

I had the first inkling that my foster mother did not love me when I was between the ages of 4 -6 years old.

People who were not family members kept telling me that my foster mother did not love me as she had picked me up from the rubbish dump. What they said troubled me, but there was no way for me to confirm it as my foster mother would always answer my queries about my identity with a curt: 'Don't ask'.

That was exactly how my foster mother answered me when I asked her why I was not given a share of the inheritance.

My foster mother kept my adoption as a big secret from me. I dared not ask any of my relatives because I knew they would tell my foster mother about it, and I would surely get into trouble with her.

## Chapter 3

# My Search for Truth

It was the practice of my foster mother to clean up Mr Khor's tombstone on All Souls' Day. My foster mother would bring me along whenever she went to clean up Mr Khor's tombstone.

On one such visit, I read Mr Khor's tombstone. I found out that on the tombstone was carved, in chronological order, all the names of the children of his three wives, but my name was not to be found. Yet, against all odds, I still harboured a hope that somehow my name was missed out accidentally.

Can you imagine how I felt at the event of the distribution of the Khor's inheritance? It was a confirmation that I was not a member of the Khor's household!

My hope was further shattered when my eldest biological brother, who was then my cousin, sought me out to inform me that I was his biological sister.

Both the above events took place when I was a teenager. As a teenager, I was already going through the normal developmental cycle of seeking my identity. These two negative events complicated my sense of identity.

## Chapter 4

# Why was I Adopted?

My aunt Sarah revealed a truth about my adoption that I had never known. I was chosen to fill the void left by my foster mother's deceased daughter. This daughter, I learned, had passed away between the ages of five and seven, during her early school years. The exact timing between her death and my adoption remains unclear to me.

Sarah explained that tuberculosis had claimed the young girl's life, a disease that was widespread in the 1900s. The story became even more complex when I learned of my foster maternal grandmother's role in my placement. She had specifically requested that my foster mother adopt me for two interconnected reasons: first, to keep me within our existing family circle, as both my foster mother and biological mother had been adopted by her; and second, to help heal the profound loss of my foster mother's child.

Hence, my foster mother had a high expectation of me to be like her daughter, who was said to be docile and submissive.

Unfortunately, for both my foster mother and I, my personality was 180 degrees different from my foster mother's deceased daughter. I was always asking questions, which my foster mother, being a typical Cantonese lady considered me to be talking back to elders, which is a definite NO, NO in the Chinese culture. Consequently, my relationship with my foster mother was a most unpleasant one.

For the readers' information my foster mother also had another biological child ie a son. He was my foster mother's second child.

# Chapter 5

# More Identity Crisis

I had confusion when I was instructed to address my Khor's relatives as:

    a.    The first wife of Mr Khor as 'big mother'. The second wife of Mr Khor as 'second mother' and my foster mother as 'mother'.

Incidentally, I had never met 'second mother ' as she did not stay in Kuala Lumpur where all the members of Khor family stayed. She stayed in Penang, which is up north of Malaysia.

    b.  The children of Mr Khor's three wives as 'first sister, second sister, third sister, fourth sister, first brother, second brother' etc.

They were adults. Why was I instructed to address them differently?

    c.  To add further to my confusion, some of the children of my stepsisters were older than me and, they were supposed to address me as 'little' aunty.

In general, all my nieces and nephews, on the Khor side, did not address me by my title but by my name.

Consequently, while growing up in the Khor family, it was clear that I was unwanted. I also had a deep lack of identity.

# Chapter 6

# Jesus wanted Me

A t a Christian conference on Inner Healing, I received a word that I was rejected while I was still in my mother's womb.

Upon hearing that word, I wailed.

Someone prayed over me, and I saw a vision of myself in the process of going through the birth canal. In that vision, I also saw Jesus standing with His outstretched arms, waiting to receive me. I did not realise then that Jesus was healing me with a strong message that I was wanted by Him even though I was not wanted by my foster mother and the Khor family.

The following Scriptures came to my mind to confirm that Jesus indeed wanted me.

Isaiah 49:15-16 NLT.

15: *"Never! Can a mother forget her nursing child? Can she feel no love for the child she borne? But even if that were possible, I would not forget you!"*

16a: *"See, I have written your* name *on the palms of my hands."*

## Chapter 7

# My Name, My Angst

My name in Chinese meant a 'herd' of moons. I did not know that that was the meaning until I met a Mandarin speaking lady who told me that my foster mother should have given me the name that meant 'playing the piano beneath the moon.'

I was angry with my foster mother and… God. I was not even given a proper meaningful name!

## Holy Spirit's Correction

When my husband and I were teaching in Johannesburg, South Africa, the participants had asked us for the meaning of our names.

I hesitated. How can I tell them that my name meant a 'herd' of moons?

It was common knowledge that in the natural world there is only one moon!

As I hesitated, I got the following impression. The impression was, in the natural world, the moon receives her light from the sun, so now my name means I am receiving the many facets of the light of the Son, i.e. Christ Jesus. Hallelujah! Now I am very proud of my name!

# Chapter 8

# Other Expectations

I came to know that my foster mother loved to study but only received primary three education in an English medium school.

I believed that my foster mother's teachers were British nationals as Malaysia then, was under the rule of the British. As such, my foster mother had a good grip of the English language, which allowed her to read and understand the daily newspapers such as, The Straits Times.

In 1900s, Chinese girls were not given much, if any education at all. Chinese girls were expected to be married off by eighteen years of age.

Consequently, my foster mother lived her dreams of obtaining higher education through me. I was expected to do well academically, which meant I was to score A's in *all* my subjects. If I did not score all A's, I was caned. In 1900s, in the Chinese culture, caning was an acceptable means to discipline a child.

My foster mother's ability to read and understand English got me into trouble when I was in primary school. I will elaborate on that incident later in my book.

## CHAPTER 9

# Latchkey Kid

When I was in kindergarten, my foster mother rented a room in a big house that had many rooms. She worked as a ticket seller at a cinema in Kuala Lumpur i.e. Coliseum cinema, which has since been demolished.

Whenever my foster mother went to work, she would lock me in the room with a potty and sometimes with some food. I remembered that there was only one window. The window had grilles of vertical bars which were like those of a prison cell.

I used to grab the bars as I peered out to watch children playing at the space that was in front of my window. I had that image in my mind for many years. Whenever that image flashed before me, I would tear up. I am very grateful to Jesus that I had an encounter with Him, many years ago, that set me free from the negative emotions of that incident. In that encounter, Jesus took me back in time.

He led me to feel the negative emotions of deprivation, sadness and loneliness that I had experienced then. Jesus impressed upon me that He understood how I felt and asked me to hand those negative emotions to Him. I am happy to report that after that encounter with Jesus, that image has become dimmer and dimmer. Now I have to recall that image intentionally, like what I am doing now. Whenever I recall that image, I can accept that it was an unfortunate incident. I no longer feel the sting of the previous emotions. I am also able to forgive my foster mother for making me a 'latch key' kid, out of her necessity to gain a living and to protect me.

Praise the Lord for He renewed my mind over that incident!

# Chapter 10

# Trouble!

My foster mother's rented room was on land the Malaysian government sought to repossess. In exchange the Malaysian government gave my foster mother an apartment among blocks of flats in Kuala Lumpur. Those blocks of flats were the first low-cost flats that were built by the Malaysian government.

The apartments were all connected by a common corridor.

The neighbours to our right belonged to a Chinese family of many children. The neighbours to our left belonged to a Malay man who had married a Chinese wife.

I was very happy that I had friends to play with at last, until my foster mother got wind that my friends wanted to learn how to ride a bicycle and that I wanted to learn too. My foster mother told me, sternly, that if I ever dared to learn to ride a bicycle, she would break my legs. I was, of course, horrified and immediately gave up that desire and subsequently, I was forbidden to play with my friends. So even as an adult now, I still do not know how to ride a bicycle.

My Muslim neighbour baked pineapple tarts for a living. I used to help her to decorate her tarts. When I was with her, in my innocence, I poured out my woes with my foster mother to her. Unfortunately, that neighbour reported everything I told her to my foster mother. I was also forbidden to visit that Malay neighbour.

I was left by myself when foster mother went to work. By then I was in primary school and being left alone, I experienced another 'latch key' experience. To entertain myself, I took to writing a diary. I hid my diary among my pile of clothes. Unfortunately, my foster mother found my diary and read it. The result of that discovery was a barrage of angry rantings and curses from my foster mother. She labelled me as being ungrateful. What else could I do but to turn my woes inward.

# Chapter 11

# My Depression

I did not understand that by turning my woes inward, I was suppressing my feelings. My suppression of my feelings led me to experience depression.

My depression was usually triggered off when I was reprimanded, severely, by my foster mother for not performing my role as a cook, washer woman and other household chores to her level of satisfaction. Then I identified strongly with Cinderella, who was allowed to live by her stepmother because she could use Cinderella as a maid.

I had many episodes of cyclical depression and panic attacks. At thirty, I finally decided that I had to seek help, I was very weary of my depression and panic attacks. I consulted a counsellor.

According to my counsellor, depression was one side of the same coin.

The other side of the coin was anger. Anger? I vehemently disagreed with my counsellor, I was not angry, I was in despair of myself…

My counsellor also informed me that for me to continue to consult with him, I had to exercise and take antidepressants.

Both my hubby and I had misgivings about taking antidepressants. We thought, incorrectly, that by taking antidepressants we were betraying and denying Jesus' ability to heal me. Hence, we did not take the counsellor's offer to prescribe antidepressants to me. My counsellor was trained in Germany in the Gestalt school of Psychology and had the licence to prescribe drugs.

## The Bird

By nature, I was not one who exercised. What finally drove me to exercise was my hubby's insistence plus my desire to consult my counsellor again because I want to get well emotionally.

Below our block of flats, (by then we had emigrated to Singapore and stayed in a Housing Development Board flat), was a jogging track. With my husband's persistent insistence, I gathered myself together and went downstairs to walk.

Not long into my walk, a bird shitted on my head!

Boy! Did I get into a rage! I was very, very angry with God. I remember shouting at God saying: 'See I want to get well and exercise so that I can consult my counsellor and this is what I get?'

## My Depression

When I related the incident to my counsellor, he roared with laughter uncontrollably. I was chagrined. What was so funny to have a bird shitting on your head?! He said: 'See you did not agree with me that you have deep seated anger and God sent a bird to get you to be in touch with your anger!'

My counsellor again gave me strict instructions that I was to take antidepressants or else no further appointments. My hubby and I were once again ambivalent about taking antidepressants.

On the eve of my appointment, I got an impression that I did not have to take the antidepressants as Jesus was going to heal me. And instantly, I felt a lifting of heaviness over my head.

NB: *By relating the above incident, I am not suggesting that depressed persons, especially Christians, need not take antidepressants.*

*In fact, later on in my 60s, I had to take 2 years of antidepressants, prescribed by a psychiatrist. By then I had come to the end of my tethers as I was still suffering from depression. Finally, I humbled myself and heeded the wise counsel of my church elder, who was also a medical doctor.*

*That elder made arrangements for me to consult with a government -based doctor, so that I could receive subsidies. Thus, I consulted a psychiatrist.*

*Thank you, Elder Peng!*

I consulted with two different psychiatrists for about two years. On 25 November 2022, the Lord finally lifted me up from my long suffering of depression.

I am happy to report that, categorically, I am now totally free from depression. I am now a joyful person. Thank you Jesus!

I was discharged by my psychiatrist on my last visit with her. Can you guess what was the date of my discharge?

Valentines' Day 2023! Jesus has a sense of humour!

# Chapter 12

# My Religious Beliefs

My foster mother had three altars in the house:

1. Heavenly god
2. Kitchen god
3. Earth God.

I would often offer joss sticks to the god of the earth to help me get good grades for my examinations.

## Introduction to Lord Christ Jesus.

I was introduced to Jesus when I was studying in a convent secondary school.

In order, to get an extra A for my 'O' level (so that I could please my foster mother), I studied the Gospel of Luke, Knox version. It was through that study of Gospel of St Luke that I learned of Jesus. I liked him. He was so kind, something I had not experienced much. However, I did not accept Jesus as my Saviour until I was 26 years old at an evangelical meeting.

## Chapter 13

# More Mention of My Depression

I did not know that I was suffering from depression until I studied psychology in my course of occupational therapy. I was shocked that I was suffering from post-traumatic syndrome and had clinical depression.

I felt ashamed of myself. I dared not inform my foster mother, who would not be able to understand. So, I stoically soldiered on in life. I suffered from cyclical depression from teenage hood till I was 72.

My worst and longest bout of depression was from 2016 to 2022. According to St John of the Cross (16th century mystic) I was in the

Dark Nights of My Soul during 2016 to 25 November 2022. Those six years were very, very difficult years for me and my beloved husband.

During those years, I would hide myself in our master bedroom and would only move between my bed and my lazy chair. I would only leave my room for meals in the kitchen.

I suffered from lack of appetite, insomnia and constipation. I could not perform any housework except that of taking our clothes to the washing machine, hung them and folded them when the wash was done. On bad days, I could not even do that one chore. My beloved husband, Ho Hoe Sing, became a house-husband. He took up marketing and cooked for me. God bless my husband for his sacrificial care of me. Thank God we had a part-time helper who came once a week to sweep and clean our floor and toilets.

In those years, I kept asking God what was happening to me, but I received no answer. At the beginning of each of those six years, I kept asking Jesus to give me a breakthrough, which finally came on 25 November 2022. Out of my great emotional pain, I began to cry out to God like Job did in Job 3:1-3. NLT.

*"At last Job spoke, and he cursed the day of his birth. He said:*

*Let the day of my birth be erased,*

*And the night I was conceived."*

Next, I pleaded with Jesus, using His words when He was in the garden of Gethsemane, when He was agonising over His soon coming crucifixion.

## More Mention of My Depression

Matthew 26:39 (NLT)

*"He went on a little father and bowed with his face to the ground, praying:*

*My Father! If it is possible, let this cup of suffering be taken away from me."*

However, Jesus did not answer my prayer until very much later. I continued to soldier on, in great pain and very, very unsure of Jesus' care and love of me.

Then one day, I received the following impression from Jesus. He said that

I did not quote Him correctly in Matthew 26:39. I looked up that verse again.

Matthew 26:39 (NLT)

*"Yet I want your will to be done, not mine."*

I grew deeper in despair. I concluded, wrongly, that I had sinned against God so badly that He would not lift me up from my depression.

## Chapter 14

# Suicidal Thoughts

During the earlier part of my six years of dark nights I received a mental suggestion to take a particular stool to the common corridor of my apartment, stand on it, climb over the parapet and jump.

I knew at once that, that suggestion, was from the evil one. I quickly called my husband to pray over me. My husband said that we could not hide my depression from our children and friends anymore.

He informed our children and some trustworthy friends to pray for me.

I thank God that:

1. The stool, that was so vivid in my mind's eye, was no longer in the house.

2. The prayers of my children and friends were answered and I was not troubled with suicidal suggestions again.

# CHAPTER 15

# Where was Jesus?

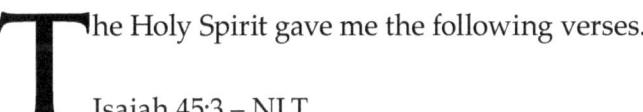

T he Holy Spirit gave me the following verses.

Isaiah 45:3 – NLT

*"And I will give you treasures hidden in the darkness – secret riches.*

*I will do this so you may know that I am the Lord, the God of Israel, the one who calls you by name."*

Hebrews 13:5b.

*"….I will never fail you. I will never abandon you."*

## My Treasures.

*First and foremost, I want to thank God for giving me a very devoted husband.*

My husband, Ho Hoe Sing, stood by me throughout those six difficult years.

I had begged him to release me and let me go home to the Lord so that he could remarry and get a better wife than me.

My husband vehemently said: 'No! I am in a *marriage covenant* with you. By the grace of God, we will go through this together.'

Against all odds my husband clung tenaciously to The Parable of the Persistent Widow:

Luke 18:1 -8 NLT

*"One day Jesus told his disciples a story to show that they should always pray and never give up. "There was a judge in a certain city," he said, "who neither feared God nor cared about people. A widow of that city came to him repeatedly, saying 'give me justice in this dispute with my enemy.' The judge ignored her for a while, but finally he said to himself, 'I don't fear God or care about people, but this woman is driving me crazy. I'm going to see that she gets justice, because she is wearing me out with her constant requests!"*

I also want to thank my daughter, Elaine, my son, Jeremy and his wife Laurencia who did not hesitate whenever my husband asked for prayer.

## Acknowledging Others

I want to acknowledge and thank people whom I know had prayed for me.

These people are my husband's colleagues and our friends from Faith Community Baptist Church, leaders and members from Zion Living Streams Community Church, my cell leader (Simon Lau and his wife, Lee Cheng), members of D'Light cell and leaders of Bethesda Bedok Tampines Church, and leaders and members of Kingdom Heart Church. Thank you again for praying for me.

## **Other Treasures.**

   a. During 2016 – 2022, by God's grace, I knew I had to read the Bible.

Jesus led me to Pastor Paul de Boutillier, Calvary Chapel, Ontario, Oregon.

Pastor Paul taught books of the Bible, verse by verse.

I had vision problems and so I listened online. I chose to listen to Pastor Paul's teachings on the books of Proverbs and Psalms as I had avoided those two books before because I had difficulty in understanding those two books.

   b. I downloaded Libby application which I used to access audio books from our national library.

   c. The best treasure, next to my husband and children, that Jesus gave me was our very, very good friends that Jesus blessed me with – the Dieus. I was lavishly touched by the Dieus' Christ- like qualities of compassion, generosity, kindness plus care. Jesus, please continue to bless Dieu and Helen!

Helen would regularly send me empathic words via WhatsApp. She did not judge me, but continued to encourage me. She was unlike other well meaning friends, who were like Job's friends in Job 2:11-13 and Job 4:1-12 NLT.

# Where was Jesus?

Job 2:11-13 NLT

*"When three of Job's friends heard of the tragedy he has suffered, they got together and travelled from their homes to comfort and console him. Their names were Eliphaz the Temanite, Bildad the Shuhite, and Zophar the Naamathite."* Job's friends started well by showing him empathy. But eventually, they were fed up with him, because he did not agree with their views about his suffering. Some of my well-meaning friends were like Job's friends. They started well by showing me empathy. Eventually, they also gave up on me when I did not snap out of my depression.

Job 4:1-12 NLT

*"Then Eliphaz the Temanite replied to Job:*

*"Will you be patient and let me say a word?*

*For who could keep from speaking out?*

*In the past you have encouraged many people;*

*you have strengthened those who were weak.*

*Your words have supported those who were falling;*

*you encouraged those with shaky knees.*

*But now when trouble strikes, you lose heart,*

*You are terrified when it touches you.*

*Doesn't your reverence for God give you confidence?*

*Doesn't your life of integrity give you hope?"*

*"Stop and think! Do the innocent die?*

*When have the upright been destroyed?*

*My experience shows that those who plant trouble and cultivate evil will harvest the same.*

*A breath from God destroys them.*

*They vanish in a blast of his anger.*

*The lion roars and the wildcat snarls, but the teeth of strong lions will be broken.*

*The fierce lion will starve for lack of prey, and the cubs of the lioness will be scattered.*

*This truth was given to me in secret, as though whispered in my ear."*

Helen once wrote to me: "Quan, there is something in you that you have yet to know. I don't know what that something is. Hang in there with Jesus."

Helen's words were a lifeline to me.

I thought to myself: If Helen had hope for me, why don't I latch on to her hope?

## Helen's friend.

Helen read a download that her friend received from Jesus.

Helen thought that her friend's download would minister to me so

Helen asked her friend for permission to forward that download to me.

I quote the download.

*"I want you to know how much I really love you. Even before I created anything out of the darkness of the world, I already had you in mind. You may not know my relationship with you started even before I laid the foundation of the world.*

*I choose you to be without any wrong and blame. That's the way I see you. You will always be perfect in my eyes. Because I formed you and conceived you, you will always be My sons and daughters.*

*You will come to enjoy this sonship through My first born Son who will bring you into the most powerful loving relationship that you will ever know.*

*Through Him, I will wash you and bath you so clean that nothing in the past will ever have a chance to interfere with My relationship with you.*

*Nothing you do in the present or future will stand in the way of Me seeing you as My perfect beloved child whom I desire to lavish My love.*

*You will come into a wholeness you have never experienced before.*

*All the anxieties, trauma, disappointments, rejection, loss, the hurts and condemnation you have ever experienced ever since you came into this imperfect world I will heal. There are things you know about and those*

*things that are buried deep in you that you do not know that are hurting you, I will redeem. You will become whole again. Free again. I have a plan for you. I will show you who you are. The gifts, talents, the special inclinations, your abilities, your beautiful personality, the richness of your character you will begin to discover for yourself how special you are and how loved you are. I will put you in places where you will be able to use all these that I have given to you. In fact, I have an even bigger plan – to bring My sons and daughters who are loved by Me, together so that they can bring this broken, hurting world which I love so much home again. I will do everything I can to help you realise your tremendous potential. But there is no need for you to strive to achieve this plan.*

*Don't strive; just rest in Me. I have sealed you with the Holy Spirit, I promised you so that you will experience me. I will really be in you and I will connect with your heart through My Spirit so that our spirits will become one. Then you will begin to understand all that I have told you and know it in your heart how much I really love you.*

*I will not coerce you. I will come to you lovingly, gently and patiently to show you all these things I have written.*

*As your heart begins to understand and know how relentless My love for you is, you will experience tremendous power. Your heart will be bursting with a new love, joy, peace, patience, kindness, goodness, faithfulness, gentleness, self- control… it will be an exhilarating journey. All those things you thought you were never be able to have and do, will come to you. I will live through you. Because I love you, you will come into an immeasurable freedom and greatness that you have never known before. That freedom and greatness was originally yours. Now I am doing a new thing in your life. I am restoring it to you the greatness and freedom you lost."*

## The Dieus' Persistence

The Dieu's visited me regularly, at least once a month, to deliver food to me and, most important of all, to pray with me.

However, I did not welcome the Dieu's' visits. Despite my rejection the Dieus' faithfully visited me. They came all the way from the west coast of Singapore to the east coast where we lived. They would ask my husband to go downstairs and prayed together (by proxy) with my husband for me.

## Malacca

Yet another good thing that the Dieus' did for me was to invite my husband and I to visit Malacca, all expenses paid for.

My immediate response to the Dieus' invitation was:

'Helen, why waste your money and your time on me? I would only hole up in the hotel room.'

Bless Helen's heart - she replied that I could do as I wish and she and her hubby will not question me. They only wanted to give me a change of environment. So, reluctantly upon my husband's reasoning with me, I accepted Helen's invitation. True to their words, the Dieus' did not question my behaviour of holing up in the hotel room.

**Dr Gary Sweeten**, ED. D – Sweeten Life Systems.

As my husband was a staff with FCBC, I was privileged to be able to attend classes conducted by Dr Gary Sweeten.

Both my husband and I learnt such topics as:

1. Connection with God, self, and others.

2. Renewed Christian Thinking.

3. Family Systems – genograms, etc.

By gaining the above knowledge, I gained some ideas how to navigate through my pain. Thank you Uncle Gary!

# Chapter 16

# Conclusion

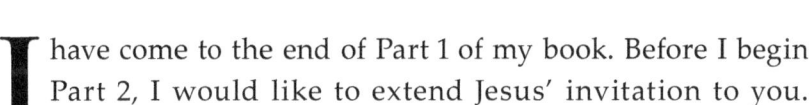

I have come to the end of Part 1 of my book. Before I begin Part 2, I would like to extend Jesus' invitation to you.

Matthew 11:28 – 30.

*"Come to me, all of you who are weary and carry heavy burdens, and I will give you rest.*

*Take my yoke upon you. Let me teach you, because I am humble and gentle at heart, and you will find for your souls.*

*For my yoke is easy to bear, and the burden I give you is light."*

Isaiah 42:3 NLT

*He (Jesus) will not crush the weakest reed*

*Or put out a flickering candle.*

*He will bring justice to all who have been wronged."*

Will you accept Jesus' invitation and give Him all your burdens?

# PART 2
# Transformation

# Chapter 1

# A Process

Exodus 23:27 – 30 NLT.

"**I will send** *my terror ahead of you and create panic among all the people whose* **lands** *you invade.* **I will** *make all your* **enemies** *turn and run.* **I will** *send terror ahead of you to drive out the* **Hivites, Canaanites,** *and* **Hittites**. **But I will not drive them out in a single year**, *because the* **land** *would become desolate and the wild animals would multiply and threaten you.* **I will drive them out a little at a time** *until your population has increased enough to take possession of the* **land**." (words in bold are mine).

**My understanding of Exodus 23: 27 -30.**

The above scriptural principle of Jesus driving out the enemies of the Israelites bit by bit is how I had and am still experiencing the transformation process that Jesus is doing in me. To me, 'land', as stated in Exodus 23:30, represents my spirit, soul and body. 'Enemy' is the evil one and the three types of enemies represent the various kind of evil that are against me. The words 'I will send' reminds me that it is **Jesus** who does the driving out of the enemies of the Israelites (and mine too) at **His Kairos** time, not at my demand. The five 'I wills' also remind me that Christ is faithful to do what He has said.

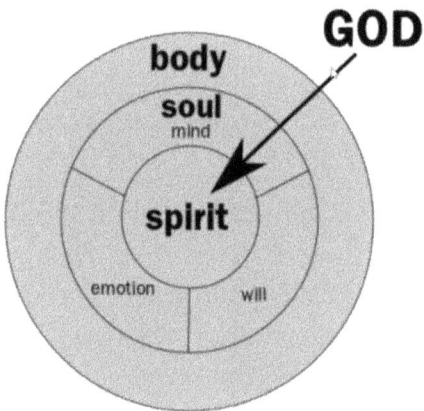

# Chapter 2

# My Beliefs

As a believer in Jesus, I believe that:

I am made of three parts:

a. Spirit b. Soul c. Body

1Thessalonians 5: 23 - 24 NLT.

*"Now may the God of peace make you holy in every way, and may your whole spirit and soul and body be kept blameless until our Lord Jesus Christ comes again. God will make this happens, for He who calls you is faithful."*

**My Spirit** (Inner Man/New Man).

My spirit is 'made alive' when I accepted Jesus as my Saviour.

Ephesians 2: 4-6 NLT.

*"But **God** is so rich in mercy, and **He** loved us so much, that even though we were dead because of our sins, **He** gave us life when **He** raised **Christ** from the dead.*

*(It is only by **God 's grace** that you have been saved!) For **He** raised us from the dead along with **Christ** and seated us with **Him** in the heavenly realms because we are united with **Christ Jesus**."* (bold and capital letters are mine).

## The Work of Lord Holy Spirit.

John 16: 5 – 9 NLT.

*"But now I am going away to the one who sent me, and not one of you is asking where I am going. Instead, you grieve because of what I've told you. But in fact, it is best for you that I go away because if I don't the* **Advocate** *(spokesman for –* Oxford dictionary) *won't come. If I do go away, then I will send **Him** to you. And when **He** comes, **He** will convict the world of its sin, and of God's righteousness, and of the coming judgement. The world's sin is that it refuses to believe in me."* (Capital and bold letters are mine).

The above verses helped me to understand that the **Lord Holy Spirit** is a 'spokesman' for me, and therefore is a Person, not a Force (which made me think of 'Star Wars' with the much repeated line of 'May the force be with you'

Another verse that helped me understand more of the work of **Lord Holy Spirit** being my 'spokesman' is:

Romans 8: 26 -28 NLT.

*"And the* **Holy Spirit** *helps us in our weakness. For example, we don't know what God wants us to pray for. But the* **Holy Spirit prays for us** *with* **groanings** *that cannot be expressed in words. And* **the Father** *who knows all hearts* **knows what the Spirit** *pleads for us believers in harmony with God's will."*

## CHAPTER 3

# My Struggle with the Holy Spirit (part 1)

I did not realise that my experiences of trying my utmost to please my foster mother had contributed to my difficulty to receive the work of the Lord Holy Spirit.

In my relationship with my foster mother, I had to tread cautiously as my survival would be at stake. I knew that my foster mother was very capable of driving me out of the house if she was very angry with me. As a consequence, I was anxiously looking for ways to please her. I did not realise that I had that *same attitude* in my relationship with our Triune God i.e. God the Father, God the Son and God the Holy Spirit. I was practising my faith by 'working' for my acceptance by our Triune God; I could not receive the truth that my salvation by Christ Jesus was by Grace, a free gift from my heavenly Father. I was to receive that gift in Faith. Hence to me, being a Christian was very burdensome; I had to apply the ten commandments strictly so that I could prove to my heavenly Father that I was worthy to be called His daughter.

## How I was Set Free.

A few days before I was set free, on 25 November 2022, the **Holy Spirit** prompted me to read the articles that were written by **Ruth Paxon.**

**Moodypublishers.com.**

Ruth Paxson (1889 – 1949) was a Bible teacher, missionary, and author. Born in Manchester, Iowa and then attended Chicago's Moody Bible Institute. She served as YWCA secretary for Iowa and eventually travelled as secretary for the Student Volunteer Movement. In 1911, Ruth sailed for the mission filed in China, sponsored by the YWCA. Health concerns forced her to leave China soon thereafter and she then taught Bible in Europe and the United States until her death. She is the author of several books, including *'Life on the Highest Plane'* and *'Caleb the Overcomer'*.

**Ruth Paxson's Articles.**

I had chanced upon Ruth Paxson when I was searching for reading materials on how to know God more. I had also downloaded and saved several of Paxson's articles on to my laptop.

# My Struggle with the Holy Spirit (Part 1)

As I obeyed the prompting of Holy Spirit to look through Paxson's articles, one article caught my attention. I am copying the article verbatim.

**Ruth Paxon: Daily Prayer:** (original)

**For the first time you are saying this prayer, say it out loud.**

*Heavenly Father, I confess my sin of unbelief that my old man had been crucified on the Cross on the day I was baptised and that I now have power in the Lord to walk in the newness of this life, his gift to me. As I confess my sin I thank you that you will forgive and cleanse me because of the blood of Jesus.*

*I know and ask the* **Lord Holy Spirit:**

1. *To* **Empower** *me with* **faith** *so that I will* **believe** *what God says in* Romans 6:6 NLT. *"We know that old sinful natures were crucified with Christ so that sin might lose its power We are no longer slaves to sin."*

**My comments on Romans 6:6**, from gleaning of Christian articles that I had read about the spiritual status of believers in Christ Jesus:

1. The Penalty of Sin has been paid for by Christ Jesus.
2. The Power of Sin has been broken by Christ Jesus.
3. The Presence of Sin is still within believers.

**Continuation of Ruth Paxson's prayer.**

1. **Empower** *me to give hearty consent to God's condemnation of and judgement upon that "old man", that "I" who are in me as*

*altogether unworthy to live and as wholly stripped of any further claim upon me.*

2. **Empower** *me with spiritual wisdom and understanding to the reality that I have both a divine and sinful nature within me.*
3. **Empower** *me to be humble and recognise the presence of my old man and the possibility of its further manifestation.*
4. **Empower** *me to choose to walk moment by moment under the Lordship of Christ and under your control today.*
5. **Empower** *me with faith to declare what God says in* 2Corinthians 5:17 New King James Version:
   *"That I am a new creation and old things have passed away."*
6. **Empower** *me today to become what I am; to put on the garment of righteousness and holiness which my heavenly Father has created in me.*
7. **Empower** *me to believe fervently that I am united with Christ in His death and resurrection and is in Christ being like Him seated in the heavenly realms at the Father's right hand.*
8. **Empower** *me with* **faith** *to stand in my new position in Christ which is the very foundation of my sanctification and of a walk in the newness of life.*
9. **Empower** *me today with* **faith** *to believe and declare that in Christ I am far above all principality, power, might and dominion so I begin the day in victory.*
10. **Empower** *me to eagerly desire every spiritual blessing that is mine in Christ by eagerly setting my affections* **primarily** *and* **pre-eminently** *upon* **heavenly things** *rather than* ***earthly things****.*

*I thank you* **Lord Holy Spirit** *that* **TODAY** *You will make Christ a living reality in me by empowering me to walk as Jesus walked in righteousness, humility, faith, obedience, lowliness, meekness, forbearance, love, patience, courage, praise and holiness.*

*I thank you for* **empowering** *me to keep* **Self** *on the* **Cross** *and* **Christ** *in the throne of my human personality.*

(NB: Numbering and bold lettering, are mine).

Paxson's daily prayer resonated with me and I repented of my sins that were stated in the prayer. After several days of asking the Lord Holy Spirit to empower me, I was set free from my six years of dark night of my soul! Thank you! Thank you, Lord Holy Spirit!

## More teachings on Holy Spirit.

After several months that I was set free from my dark nights of my soul, my hubby and I were invited to attend a church camp. At that camp, I was literally 'soaked' with several days of teaching on the Personhood of the Holy Spirit.

Father God had graciously renewed my mind over His good gift to me i.e. the Lord Holy Spirit. Thank you! Thank you, Father God.

# Chapter 4

# The Work of Holy Spirit, My Struggle (part 2)

When I was in kindergarten, primary school and secondary schools, my foster mother worked as a ticket seller at a cinema, Coliseum, in Kuala Lumpur, Malaysia.

That cinema mostly showed Malay and Indian movies. My foster mother would park me before the movie screen whenever she had to take the evening shift.

Malay 'ghost' movies were shown in Coliseum. I remembered that I sat under two such movies i.e. Pontianak and Orang Minyak.

I was terrified as I watched those movies. I closed my eyes so that I could not see the images but I could still hear the sound effects as the ghosts appeared.

Those two movies confirmed for me that ghosts were to be feared and that they would always harm me. I did not understand that my fear of ghosts had prevented me from receiving the Lord Holy Spirit until one day a fellow believer in Christ Jesus congratulated me for receiving Christ Jesus as my saviour.

She said: 'Congratulations! Now you have the Holy Ghost inside you!'

I was absolutely terrified with the lady's statement. I thought to myself. *What? Now I had the Holy 'Ghost' inside of me? No way!*

I did not want that! I was already so terrified of ghosts that were outside of me! Hence, I rejected my heavenly Father's good gift to me i.e. the Lord Holy Spirit.

I want to thank Father God for renewing my mind over my understanding of the Lord Holy Spirit. Now I am totally at peace with relating with the Lord Holy Spirit.

# Chapter 5

# Growing My Spirit Man

In May 2022, I was recommended by Pastor Lazarus, Malaysian, to attend Pastor Paul Kim's teaching on **Bible Spirit Speed Reading (BSSR).** Pastor

Lazarus conducts a six session zoom on Christ Transformation Prayer (CTP), which I had attended twice. Pastor Lazarus recommended that in order to maintain the freedom that I had gained through CTP, I needed to learn about BSSR.

## BSSR

To explain what BSSR is, I am copying verbatim some points that I had downloaded from Pastor Lazarus' power points. Pastor Lazarus has given me permission to quote his points.

## Points on BSSR.

1. BSSR is not Bible Study but reading chapters of Bible book, like soaking in God's word. If the Lord reveals or expose your negative emotion, you then can use prayer to remove them. I would like to add my understanding to the above statement by Pastor Lazarus by including Dr. Gary's 6S's from his book Rational Christian Thinking, renewing the mind.

   The six S's are: Spot, Stop, Stand, Send, Supplant, Seek spiritual help.

2. Matthew 4:4 New Kings James.

   The Word of God is spiritual food for my spirit man.

   *"But He answered and said it is written, Man shall not live by bread alone, but by every word that proceeds from the mouth of God."*

3. Matthew 12:43 – 45 New Kings James.

   *"When an unclean spirit goes out of a man, he goes through dry places, seeking rest, and finds none. Then he says, 'I will return to my house from which I came.' And when he comes, he finds it empty, swept, and put in order. Then he goes and takes with him seven other spirits more wicked than himself, and they enter and dwell there; and the last state of that man is worse than the first. So shall it also be with this wicked generation."*

## My Cyclical Depression

During my six years of dark nights of my soul, I consistently asked the Lord what was happening to me. The Lord did not answer me until I was delivered out of my deep depression. The Lord Holy Spirit gave me revelation to the above Scriptures. I then understood that my many experiences of deliverance by the Lord were real. I did feel light and happy after each deliverance. However, the good feelings lasted for about 6 months and then they were gone. I was very puzzled and confused. Due to my experiences with my foster mother, which had caused me to feel anxious whenever I perceived that I had failed her, I thought that I had failed the Lord too. I felt condemned and ashamed of myself. I stopped telling others that the Lord had delivered me out of my depression as I felt guilty that I had lied. The revelation that was given to me by the Lord set me free from my self- condemnation.

Ephesians 5:18 Contemporary English Version.

*"Don't destroy yourself by getting drunk, but let the Spirit fill your life."*

My house was empty because I did not let the Lord Holy Spirit to fill me and I also did not read the Bible regularly nor memorise Scriptures.

I repented of my sins that the Holy Spirit revealed to me. I resolved to read the Bible more regularly; spending time to highlight the verses that spoke to me and making notes at the edge of the pages of the Bible. I prefer listening so I used audio Bible (at speed 2) as I read along. I was practicing BSSR.

Four points from Pastor Kim:

'When you do BSSR it is your spirit man receiving the WORD through the Holy Spirit and your spirit man is strengthened and edified.'

At the point of my being 'born' again, my spirit man is a baby, just like a newly born human baby. Next, I learned that just as a newborn baby required milk to grow so likewise my baby spiritual man need milk to grow. 1Peter 2: 2-5 NLT.

1Peter 2: 2-5 NLT.

*"Be like newborn babies who are thirsty for the pure spiritual milk that will help you grow and be saved."*

Pastor Kim said that just as a physical newborn did not question his mother about the milk, she was feeding him, but instead take it eagerly, I needed to practice BSSR in faith. I was not supposed to 'think or analyse'.

Pastor Kim said that highly 'intellectual' people would have difficulty to practice BSSR. He also commented that we, Singaporeans, would face the issue of just 'listening' to the Word of God and stop analysing what we are doing as we practise BSSR.

1Corinthians 14:15 New Kings James.

*"What is the conclusion then? I will pray with the spirit, and I will also pray with understanding. I will sing with the spirit, and I will also sing with understanding."*

## My Benefits from Practising BSSR.

Ephesians 1:13 – 14 NLT.

*"And now you Gentiles have also heard the truth, the Good News that God saves you. And when you believed in Christ, he identified you as his own by giving you the Holy Spirit, whom he promised long ago. The Spirit is God's guaranteed that he will give us an inheritance he promised and that he has purchased us to be his own people. He did this so we would praise and glorify him."*

The truth of verse 14, finally hit home when I did BSSR on the book of Ephesians, it did not hit me when I did a Bible study on Ephesians.

When I caught that truth in my spirit man, I was set free from my yearning to be given a share of Khor's family inheritance as an acknowledgement that I was a member of the Khor family. I repented of my lust to be included and accepted by the Khor family when, in reality, I am now in God's family through the blood of Jesus, I have spiritual blessings which are far better than the physical blessings that I had yearned for.

Galatians 5:22 – 23 NLT.

*"But the Holy Spirit produces this kind of fruit in our lives: love, joy, peace, patience, kindness, gentleness, and self-control. There is no law against these things."*

I learned from Pastor Kim that as I consciously sow to the Holy Spirit through BSSR I would be reaping His fruit. And that was very true for me. I no longer felt depressed but felt love, joy and peace! Thank you, Father God for giving me Your good gift of the Lord Holy Spirit.

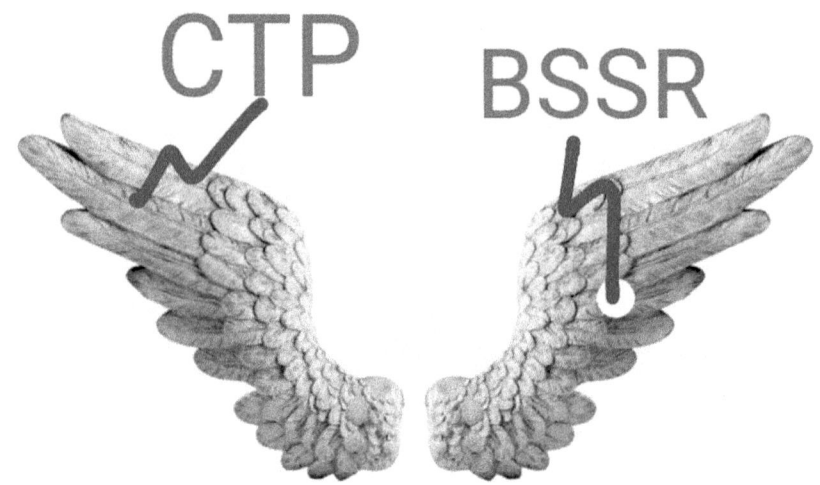

## Chapter 6

# My Soul

My soul also has 3 parts i.e. my thinking, my emotions and my will.

**More information about my soul.**

When I read Christian literature, I learned that, originally, my spirit is to control my soul which then controls my body. However, that order is reversed now because of my fallen sin nature.

The reverse order would be:

My body controls my soul (my thinking, feeling and will). Next, my soul would affect my spirit/mood. Before Jesus delivered me from my past, my body controlled my soul which in turn controlled my spirit.

Allow me to explain my last statement.

Previously, whenever my body did not feel well, my emotion (my soul) I would feel either anxious or worried and my thinking (soul) would be negative, like, do I have this or that disease?

Next, my will (soul) could either be strong or weak in assessing what to do the condition of my body. I could choose to admit or deny my negative emotion (anxiety, fear etc) with regards to the status of my body.

The combination of the three parts of my soul i.e. thinking, emotion and will, would influence my decision of what to do with the status of my body, i.e. to consult /not to consult a doctor.

**Life Skill** (Dr Gary Sweeten).

I learned a life skill, from Dr Gary Sweeten, on how I could *process* and *reflect* on what is happening to me at a given situation. Gary's life skill enabled me to *respond* rather than to *react* to my situation.

I shall attempt to summarise the Life Skill that is well written by Dr. Gary in his book: Rational Christian Thinking, renewing the mind).

I attended a workshop where Dr Gary taught life skill in the form of:

1. **A**ctivating event.
2. **B**elief System.
3. **C**onsequential Feeling.
4. **D**ecisive Action (ABCD).

Dr Gary did a role play which helped me to understand ABCD of an emotion. In the role play, Dr Gary had two participants involved. After briefing them on what to do, Dr Gary asked one the participants (X) to walk as though he was walking in a garden. Next, Dr Gary threw a toy snake onto the floor.

When X saw the snake, X ran away, with his face showing fear.

Then Dr Gary removed the toy snake and asked the second participant, Y, to walk in the 'garden'. Dr Gary threw the same toy snake onto the floor.

Y did not run away but instead he went nearer, cautiously, to the snake, as if to take a closer look.

That role play helped me to understand A*B*CD of an emotion. But I still could not understand *B* (belief system).

Dr Gary helped me to understand **B** when he asked X and Y, respectively, why each of them did what they did.

X explained that he was afraid that the snake might attack him. X added further that his father was bitten by a snake once and his father had to be rushed to the hospital.

Y explained that he knew, from his reading of Nature articles, that not ALL snakes were dangerous therefore he was curious to find out more. From the explanations of X and Y, I gained understanding of what Belief System is all about.

Dr Gary gave further explanation of ABCD.

He said that, normally, ABCD of an emotion, initially, did not seem to occur to in the sequence of ABCD.

In reality, the sequence appeared to be:

A - C – D. B seemed to be missing.

To my understanding the sequence of A-C-D illustrated my *reaction* to an

Activating event (A).

In the role play that Dr Gary carried out, the **A**ctivating event was the appearance of the toy snake.

So, how and when do I get in touch with my **B** (belief system)?

Dr Gary explained that in order to find the **Belief** system that was driving my *emotion,* I had to calm down. When I was calm, I was then able to reflect on my *reaction* to the **A**ctivating event.

## Diaphragm Breathing.

I learned how to calm myself through diaphragm breathing at one workshop that I attended.

## My Soul

In that workshop, I was instructed to put my palms on to my tummy.

Next, I was to breathe in as though I was inflating a balloon.

In that process, my tummy will push my palms up. I was instructed to hold that posture for a count of 3/5 before I gradually released air from my tummy, as though I was deflating a balloon. As I gradually released air, I could feel the descent of my palms.

If I needed to, I could repeat the above actions, as many times as I wished. I found that diaphragm breathing helped me to relax. I could calm down.

In my calmness, I could analyse the whole succession of quick events that had happened.

1Peter 1:13 – 16 NLT.

*"So prepare your minds for action and exercise self-control. Put all your hope in the gracious salvation that will come to you when Jesus Christ is revealed to the world. So you must live as God's obedient children. Don't slip back into your old says of living to satisfy your own desires. You didn't know any better then. But now you must be holy in everything you do, just as God who chose you is holy. For the Scriptures say," You must be holy because I am holy."*

Leviticus 11:44 – 45 NLT.

*"For I am the Lord your God. You must consecrate yourselves and be holy, because I am holy. So do not defile yourselves with any of these small animals that scurry along the ground. For I, the Lord, am the who brought*

*you up from the land of Egypt, that I might be your God. Therefore, you must be holy because I made holy."*

I had read from several articles by mature Christians that to us, believers of Christ Jesus, Egypt was our old ways of doing things. These authors also wrote that it was easy for God to take us up from Egypt but to get Egypt out of us was a different story.

As a believer in Christ Jesus, I had to decide to cooperate with Christ Jesus to get Egypt out of me i.e. my old ways of thinking which led me to ungodly behaviour. To accomplish that decision, I had to read the Bible and let the Word reveal to me what my ungodly thinking and behaviour were. Next, I had to repent of my ungodly thinking and behaviour. I also had to be humble and asked Holy Spirit to empower me to change those ungodly thoughts and behaviour to godly behaviour that were stated in the bible.

John 15:5 NLT.

*"Yes, I am the vine; you are the branches. Those who remain in me, and I in them, will produce much fruit. For apart from me you can do nothing."*

Jesus gave me a vivid physical understanding of the vine and branchprinciple when I was in Kazakhstan at a Kazak's home. In that home I saw a big cluster of grapes that were attached to the vine.

The attachment of me to Jesus, my vine, is the work of Lord Holy Spirit.

# Chapter 7

## My body

My body is the physical part of me which has 5 senses:

a. Touch b. Smell. c. Sight. d. Taste. e. Hear

My 5 senses help me to understand my physical world.

When I was a child, I did not exercise. For fruits, I only ate bananas and papayas, as my foster mother could not afford apples, oranges, and grapes.

After our marriage and before Christ Jesus transformed me, I also did not eat apples, oranges, grapes, and durian! This was due to my imprint that I was not worthy of such 'luxuries'.

I used to quarrel with my hubby whenever he bought those fruits, especially durians which are expensive.

I want to thank Lord Christ Jesus that after he has transformed me, I am now able to buy 'luxury' fruits for myself. The very first 'luxury' fruit that I bought for myself was …Durian!

I also want to thank Lord Christ Jesus that currently my hubby and I are joining communities to exercise 2/3 time per week. We do stretching, building up muscles and Zumba.

# Chapter 8

# My Role

In my journey of transformation by Lord Christ Jesus, I realised that I had to be *proactive* and *cooperate* with the Lord Holy Spirit. It was of utmost importance to obey Jesus' teaching in the following areas:

1. Forgiveness. 2. Confession of sins. 3. Repentance.
4. Blessing my enemies.

## 1. Forgiveness.

Among the many facets of Forgiveness, I have learned the following

Forgiveness is:

    a. **My Choice**.

Matthew 18:32-33 (NLT); Parable of the Unforgiving Debtor.

*"Then the king called in the man he had forgiven and said, 'You evil servant! I forgave you that tremendous debt because you pleaded with me. Shouldn't you have mercy on your fellow servant, just as I had mercy on you?"*

    b. **A Process** of forgiving the perpetrator/s many times.

Matthew 18:21 -22. NLT.

*"Then Peter came to him (Jesus) and asked, 'Lord, how often should I forgive someone who sins against me? Seven times?' 'No, not seven times, Jesus replied, seventy times seven."'*

That's what my heavenly Father will do to you ***if you refuse to forgive*** your brothers and sisters ***from your heart.***(bold emphasis is mine.)'

    c. **Forgive from the heart**.

Matthew 18:35 NLT.

*"That's what my heavenly Father will do to you if you refuse to forgive your brothers and sisters from your heart."*

I did not fully understand what it meant to 'forgive from my heart' until the Lord Holy Spirit gave me revelation. If I had forgiven my foster mother from my heart, I would not avoid her. I would have compassion on her for she was also trapped in culture and traditions and she did not know the Lord Jesus Christ nor had the gift of the Lord Holy Spirit to empower her to change her expectations of me.

### d. Why won't I forgive?

The main reason why I would not forgive is my great need for justice. I kept thinking to myself – this and that my foster mother did to me was not fair.

I finally decided to forgive my foster mother when the Lord Holy Spirit led me to the following verse.

Romans 12:19 – 21 NLT.

*"Dear friends, never take revenge. Leave that to the righteous anger of God. For the Scriptures say, 'I will take revenge; I will pay them back.' Says the Lord.*

*Instead, 'If your enemies are hungry, feed them.*

*If they are thirsty, give them something to drink.*

*In doing this, you will heap burning coals of shame on their head.'*

*Don't let evil conquer you, but conquer evil by doing."*

Deuteronomy 32:35 NLT.

*"I will take revenger; I will pay them back. In due time their feet will slip. Their day of disaster will arrive, and their destiny will overtake them."*

e. **Give God your Revenge** (Pastor John Piper, desiringgod.org).

I had always thought that by my withholding my forgiveness my FM would be hurt. I found out from other Christian literature that I was actually poisoning myself! Pastor John's teaching settled my reluctance to forgive my foster mother. I wanted to stop poisoning myself.

f. **Forgiving Myself**

One aspect of forgiveness that was alien to me was that of forgiving myself for making bad choices. (Love your neighbour as yourself. Mark 12:31.)

I could not fully understand Mark 12:31 until I went for a one-day silent retreat.

In that retreat, I was guided by a spiritual director, who gave me scriptures to meditate upon. I stayed in a room all myself. The room was like a hotel room with a single bed and attached bathroom. I was also to have lunch alone; absolutely no talking. At 5pm, I met with my spiritual director and I gave her report of my experience and my goal for the future.

In my conversation with my spiritual director, I informed her of the following:

John 5:14 – NLT. (Jesus heals a man who had been sick for 38 years)

My spiritual director responded to my report by asking me what I thought about Jesus' instructions to the sick man i.e. "Now you are well; so stop sinning, or something even worse may happen to you."

## My Role

My reply to my spiritual director was that when I asked Jesus what sin must I stop doing?

Jesus replied: Stop hating yourself.

Next, my spiritual director asked me if I knew what was the opposite of hating oneself. I gingerly replied: Loving yourself?

My spiritual director affirmed my reply. Then my spiritual director asked me how was I going to love myself?

This time I confidently showed her my recent new purchase – an 11 inch pink teddy bear!

I had bought that teddy bear, with much ambivalence, just before I attended my silent retreat. And why was that purchase considered as part of my selfcare?

As a child the only toys I had was a kerosene stove and a dining table with six chairs.

When we shifted from our one room rental to our low-cost government flat, my foster mother would not allow me to bring those toys, her rationale being that I was too old to have toys. By overcoming my ambivalence to buy the pink teddy bear, I was putting into practice what a counsellor instructed me to do i.e. parent myself since my foster mother did not parent me.

    g. **Not a Denial**

I had to give myself permission to acknowledge negative events instead of sweeping them under the carpet.

It was difficult for me to accept that the negative events had happened between my foster mother as I was trapped in a bind that involved the cultural teaching that elders were always right and that I, as a junior, cannot speak against elders and my internal pain.

It took me quite a while to overcome the cultural expectation of my role towards my foster mother and could finally 'talk' to her in the presence of Jesus that she had abused me physically and emotionally. I came to understand that the above process is known as Inner Healing, where my soul was being healed of its wounds by Jesus.

# Inner Healing Experiences.

During the Inner Healing process, I experienced and expressed my negative emotions to Jesus plus also chose to give those emotions to Him.

Next, there was a divine exchange. Jesus gave me His empathy and His peace.

What a blessing it was to go to Jesus!

Song: What a Friend we have in Jesus by Alan Jackson.

## A Memorable Experience.

I attended a five-day workshop on Inner Healing that was conducted by Pastor Joseph Ozawa, American born Japanese. At the end of the workshop. Pastor Ozawa released a word of knowledge that 'some of you here were rejected while you were in your mother's womb'. Upon hearing that word, I wailed uncontrollably. When the workshop ended, I told a sister-in-Christ about what had happened. She prayed over me, and I had a mental picture of me coming out of the birth canal. Jesus was standing outside with His outstretched hands, waiting to receive me.

Isaiah 49: 14-16 NLT.

> 14. *"Yet Jerusalem says, 'The Lord has deserted us: the Lord has forgotten us'."*
>
> 15. ***"Never! Can a mother forget her nursing child? Can she feel no love for the child she had borne?***
>
>    ***But even if that were possible,***
>
>    ***I would not forget you!"***

16. *"See, I have written your name on the palms of my hands."*

(Bold letters are mine).

However, I could not receive the truths of v15 -16 until many years later, after many more inner healing sessions by Jesus. Today, I can *confidently* and *wholeheartedly* embrace those truths. *I am loved by Jesus!*

## Follow up of Experience.

After the above inner healing experience, Pastor Ozawa, conducted a similar workshop for the staff of Faith Community Baptist Church (FCBC). I had the privilege of attending that workshop as my husband was a pastor with Faith Community Baptist Church (FCBC).

As I listened to Pastor Ozawa's teaching, I grew more and more perturbed within me. I knew I had to be ministered to by Pastor Ozawa. I wished for the day, when Pastor Ozawa would announce that he would minister to the participants who wanted to be ministered, would come sooner.

When the day of ministry came, it was a Friday, Pastor Ozawa called me out and I wailed uncontrollably. Pastor Ozawa told the participants to leave me alone for the Lord Holy Spirit to do His work with me.

However, the Lord Holy Spirit had not finished His work with me on that Friday. He continued His work the following day (Sat) in my home. I woke up at 6am and I just had the urge to cry. It was like a tap was turned on from within me and I cried and cried. I

## My Role

could not understand what was happening to me. I had no control. I told my husband to give me a box of tissue. I put pieces of tissue under my face and I laid on my side to cry. I was too tired to keep on wiping my tears. That day I had bought three tickets for the play Toy Soldier. I bought three tickets only as my husband had to work on Saturday. I requested my husband not to work overtime so that he could take the children to the play. My husband agreed. I also asked my husband to ask Pastor Ozawa what was happening to me.

When my husband went to work, I continued to cry.

Then my two children began to play on the piano the song, "Beauty and the Beast". When I heard that song, I wailed upon hearing the word "Beast" because that was what I felt about myself.

Side note:

*[Even as I am typing this segment of my book now, 23 November 2024, my phone is playing the song Beauty and the Beast! Now I am weeping with tears of gladness because I feel like a Beauty, no longer a Beast! Hallelujah! Thank you! Thank you Jesus!]*

I continued crying until 6pm. Promptly at 6pm I stopped crying. It was like the tap inside me was turned off. I tried to cry but was unsuccessful. I could not fully embrace the above healing experience. I was good for some months after the experience but went into depression not too long after that.

When I went into depression, I was confused. I thought I had betrayed Jesus. I felt condemned. I felt ashamed of myself. By the grace of Christ Jesus, I got understanding of what was happening to me when I attended Dr. Gary's workshop (written in chapter 10).

## Inner Healing Ministries.

For Inner Healing sessions, I went to *Elle Ministries* ( founder is Peter Horrobin) and *Restoring the Foundations* (founders are Chester and Betsy Kylstra). I was also ministered to by *Pastor Lazarus,* Malaysian, in *his Christ Transforming Prayer.* Pastor Lazarus conducts six sessions on zoom.

## Chapter 9

# Jesus is a Safe Person

As I grew to be in touch with my reactions and feeling, I also grew to know that Jesus is a safe person to download all my negative emotions. Nothing I had ever felt or said in His presence shocked Him.

It was much later in my journey with Jesus that I knew that when He came as a man, He felt all the negative emotions mankind has ever felt.

Allow me to explain. Generally, human emotions can be categorised as:

## Mad, Sad, Glad and Scared.

(https://jennynurick.com/four-basic-emotions-mad-sad-glad-and-scared/)

According to my understanding Jesus felt:

1. **Sadness** when Judas betrayed him – Mark 14:44-46 NLT.

*"The traitor, Judas, had given them a prearranged signal: 'You will know which one to arrest when I greet him with a kiss. Then you can take him away under guard.'"*

2. **Gladness** – John 4: 39 NLT.

*"Many Samaritans from the village believed in Jesus because the woman had said, 'He told me everything I ever did!'"*

3. **Mad** when the Pharisees rejected Him.

4. **Scared** when He had to go to Calvary to be hung.

To me Jesus was the perfect empathiser.

# Chapter 10

# Forgiving God

When I came across the concept of forgiving God, I had difficulty to accept it. I thought to myself: who was I, the created to 'forgive' the Creator of me.

I was helped with my struggle when I read the following article

https://founders.org/articles/forgiving-god/

# Chapter 11

# Limbic Lag

*3 Steps Forward, 2 Steps Back*

Dr. Gary has written in length about Limbic lag on his book Rational Christian Thinking; renewing the mind.

Excerpts from Dr Gary's book -with his permission, on **Limbic lag** (chapter 6 :1-2).

*"Though there are many features of the brain that impact the rational thinking process, for our purposes we shall examine only two, the neocortex and the limbic system. This will help to understand why emotional habits are difficult to change.*

*The neocortex is the analytical center of the brain which takes in data and stores it in it's 'files', a process which is much like programming a computer. This information is recorded and stored for use at any time but is not combined with any feelings.*

*The limbic system is the feeling center of the brain. It is located deep within the cranial cavity and produces feeling responses to the data recorded by the neocortex. There are no feelings in the neocortex. However, these two parts of the brain are partners which work together to receive and process perceptions, memory, values, beliefs, and attitudes, and to develop feeling responses. In a simplistic way we state that the neocortex takes in factual data and the limbic system produces feelings.*

*If you were driving down an interstate highway one clear, sunny afternoon and happened to glance into the rear-view mirror to discover the image of a black and white police cruiser gaining on you rapidly with its red and blue lights flashing and its siren screaming, you have a great example of how the neocortex and the limbic system work together. The neocortex takes in the data:*

*Neocortex*

*. black and white automobile*

*. red and blue lights flashing*

*. approaching from the rear*

*. moving at high speed*

*. siren sounding*

*All these neutral images would immediately be mixed with memories as well as other simultaneously collected information in the neocortex.*

# LIMBIC LAG

. *your speed right now*

. *the speed limit*

. *your speed a few miles ago*

. *past experiences with police.*

. *perceptions of police.*

*Your neocortex data-processing center analyses the data, reaches a conclusion, and sends your limbic system the message.*

*Your limbic (feeling) response will vary according to your perceptions and Belief System. You could feel great because you saw a drunk driver pass you driving at a high rate of speed, and you believe that the police car is after him. You may feel fear and anxiety even though your speed and driving decorum are well within the acceptable limits of the law.*

*The neocortex could have received and recorded all of the data necessary to inform the limbic system of the reality that you had, in fact, broken no law and yet you could have a feeling response as though the police car were coming for you. You know the facts but the feelings are the same. This phenomena is termed limbic lag.*

*In the process of renewing the mind and developing new habits of thought, belief, and feelings, the concept of limbic lag can be encouraging. The limbic system lags behind. With the inclusion of new details into the neocortex, new situations that we know are right will 'still feel as though they are not."*

# Chapter 12

# Progressive Sanctification

I had to re-read Limbic lag several times before I finally could understand and accept it.

Excerpt from Dr Gary's book, with his permission - Rational Christian Thinking, chapter 8 -2.

*"The emphasis here is on what we term "progressive sanctification", which means that we are to grow progressively more mature in Christ from the point of justification (being born again) throughout our entire lives, even until physical death. Although we can achieve substantial healing and wholeness in Christ while on this earth, absolute perfection will not occur until we have been resurrected and are seated with Christ in heaven.*

*As we grow daily in maturity and become more like our Lord, the nature of our temptation itself will never be completely gone from our lives. In fact, Hebrew 4:15 says that Jesus Himself was tempted then it is clear that we shall also be tempted. So, although the temptations of the flesh may not have the strength they once did, the temptations of the spirit, which are more subtle, may be even more devastating to our life. These temptations include spiritual pride, manipulation, power, greed, and selfishness. All of us know the power of the evil one in these areas and need to learn how to resist the temptations that would draw us into sin. However, most temptations arise from within our own hearts rather than from an outside force, such as Satan. As Pogo says, 'we have met the enemy and he is us.'"*

Dr Gary's teaching on limbic lag and progressive sanctification helped me to be merciful and gracious to myself. I remembered that Helen often told, 'Quan, you are too harsh on yourself.'

Unbeknownst to me, I had internalised my foster mother's high expectation on to me and I was also having high expectation of myself. The reason why I had cyclical depression was, besides the spiritual one I did not welcome the Lord Holy Spirit plus I did not read or meditate on Scriptures consistently, that whenever I went into depression again after my very real deliverance from the Lord, out of my confusion, I judged myself. I also felt that I had betrayed the Lord Christ Jesus as I had triumphantly declared to my friends that He had delivered me out of my depression. Soon, I stopped declaring to my friends and I worked harder to overcome my depression, but alas it was to no avail. Consequently, as Pogo stated I was my own enemy and I entered into a vicious cycle of Shame, Guilt, Blame and Self-condemnation.

Romans 7:14 -25 NLT.

## Progressive Sanctification

"So the trouble is not with the law, for it is spiritual and good. The trouble is with me, for I am all too human, a slave to sin. I don't really understand myself, for I want to do what is right, but I don't do it. Instead, I do what I hate. But if I know that what I am doing is wrong, this shows that I agree that the law is good. So I am not the one doing wrong; it is sin living in me that does it (this reminded me of Ruth Paxson's point that as a believer in Christ Jesus, I had both the sinful and divine nature within me). And I know that nothing good lives in me, that is, in my sinful nature. I want to do what is right, but I can't. I want to do what is good, but I don't. I don't want to do what is wrong, but I do it anyway. But if I do what I don't want to do, I am not really the one doing wrong; it is sin living in me that does it.

I have discovered this principle of life-that when I want to do what is right, I inevitably do what is wrong. I love God's law with all my heart. But there is another power within me that is at war with my mind. This power makes me a slave to the sin that is still within me. Oh, what a miserable person I am! Who will free me from this life that is dominated by sin and death? Thank God! The answer is in Jesus Christ our Lord. So, you see how it is: In my mind I really want to obey God's law, but because of my sinful nature I am a slave to sin."

I struggled to understand the above Scriptures for many years. My contention was: Paul was putting the blame on sin that was living inside me therefore I was not to be blamed when I did not do what I wanted to do. To me, that was irresponsibility, something I struggled to accept.

I received further understanding of the above Scriptures from Dr Gary's teaching in his book Rational Christian Thinking, renewing the mind (chapter 8-1).

*"A universal facet of the Christian life is that none of us lives without the daily problem of temptation. As babes in Christ, our temptations may attempt to draw us toward the gross besetting sins of our "before Christ" days. For example. We may struggle with sexual promiscuity, alcohol abuse, destructive anger, stealing or lying. These are the obvious and overt sins of the flesh, and we can clearly see the need to resist the temptation that would draw us into those thoughts and acts.*

*As we become more mature, however, the obvious manifestations of the old nature are slowly relinquished as their root causes are cut away and the Holy Spirit begins to develop His fruit within us. Unfortunately, the more subtle temptations to sin are ever present in our human nature to draw us away from a life of holiness, Paul was an articulate Christian of maturity when he wrote in Romans 7 that even he knew what was right in his mind, he found that the law of sin still dwelled in his mortal flesh (the old nature of the deep heart that still had the residue of bondage, rebellion, guilt* and *shame). Paul then notes that only Christ, not our works, can deliver us from this bondage of the flesh (Romans 7:24-25). Thus, the great Apostle Paul continued to struggle with temptation long after he has been called and equipped to be a missionary and an apostle. The exact nature of this sin might have changed from blatant outbursts of anger to more subtle forms of fleshly behaviour, but he continued to be tempted, and he continued to sin. In Philippians 3:12-16 he also notes that it is his goal to live in the power of the resurrected Christ, but it is clear that he had not yet reached his goal of sinless perfection. He then advises us to forget that which is behind, keep our eyes on the goal, and put all of our strength in accomplishing that goal."*

# CHAPTER 13

# Confession of Sins

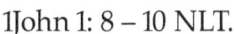

1John 1: 8 – 10 NLT.

"*If we claim we have no sin, we are only fooling ourselves and not living in the truth. But if we confess our sins to him, he is faithful and just to forgive us our sins and to cleanse us from all wickedness. If we claim we have not sinned, we are calling God a liar and showing that his word has place in our hearts."*

After the Lord set me free from my bondage to depression, I realised that I had sinned against Him in so many ways. I had to go through a season of confessing my sins to Him, often time in the presence of my husband:

James 5:16 -18 NLT.

*"Confess your sins to each other and pray for each other so that you may be healed. The earnest prayer of a righteous person has great power and produces wonderous results. Elijah was as human as we are, and yet when he prayed earnestly that no rain would fall, none fell for three and a half years! Then, when he prayed again, the sky sent down rain and the earth began to yield its crops."*

Matthew 18:18-20 NLT.

*"I tell you the truth, whatever you forbid on earth will be forbidden in heaven, and whatever you permit on earth will be permitted in heaven. I also tell you this: If two of you agree here on earth concerning anything you ask, my Father in heaven will do it for you. For where two or three gather together as my followers, I am there among them."*

I want to thank Father God for giving me my husband, Ho Hoe Sing, who has great compassion on my emotional state. He soldiered stoically with me in my cyclical depressions, even when I begged him to let go of me when I was in my six years of dark nights of my soul. Thank you, my dearest hubby!

Then I had to stand firm on His promise that He will forgive me of my sins and cleanse me from all wickedness. I also had to continuously call on the Lord Holy Spirit to help me to repent - stop thinking ungodly thoughts especially those that make me doubt the character of God.

I read from articles by mature believers in Christ that both confession of sins and repentance are gifts from our heavenly Father. My human nature is such that I would not confess and repent voluntarily.

## Confession of Sins

Genesis 6:5 NLT.

*"The Lord observed the extent of human wickedness on the earth, and he saw that everything they thought or imagined was consistently and totally evil."*

My understanding of the above Scripture is that I cannot boast of **My** acceptance of Christ Jesus; it is the grace of heavenly Father who led me to His son.

John 6.44 NLT.

*"For no one can come to me unless the Father who sent me draws them to me, and at the last day I will raise them up."*

# Chapter 14

# Repentance

*Must one need to apologise before one can qualify to repent?*

## Excerpt of a blog from Reddit.com.

One family member is asking me to forgive another family member who has hurt me repeatedly. The family member has not said she is sorry ever and continues to hurt me. Do I need to forgive her, Biblically speaking? My perspective is that even God does expect salvation without our repentance. I know Jesus said to forgive 70 times seven, but he also said that within the context of a story where those in the parable begged for a debt to be cancelled. Yes, we need to love mercy, but what about the seeking justice part? Thanks for any and all perspectives

*...Edit: please cite where you're referring to in Scripture so I can read it for perspective. Additional edit: the offending party is not a believer.*

## Comments from:

### a. Informed Conservative (2years ago).

*If you want to be forgiven, you have to forgive. There is such a thing as righteous anger, but forgiving others is different from being angry... Living life with rage is like drinking poison hoping that it will kill your enemy.*

*I'm very mad at a lot of people in my life, but I've forgiven them. I'm still upset about many things, but I've been working on forgiving and it has made my life better.*

*Once you hand that over to Christ and start sleeping at night, rather than dwelling on hurt, your healing will start. I am not lecturing at all. I hope that what I've said can help.*

### b. oneryarly68

*Yes, you do. Now that does not mean you forget, break bread with them or be their best buddy. But when you can pray for their salvation and forgive them for what they did to you then YOU will feel better and be free.*

### c. Sitefool.

*This is the best answer. I was gunna say before reading this: God would still love you even if you hurt him. Love is the key and with love I guess forgiveness would come. Easy words to say very very difficult to do. Forgive but definitely cut 'em off like a turd. Seems detrimental to your well being'.*

## My response to the blog.

I definitely felt that I was being 'righteous' in my anger towards my foster mother (FM). Yet I was actually drinking 'poison', thinking that it would kill my FM. On the contrary, I was killing myself. I was battling depression and all its accompanying symptoms. When I finally realised my foolishness to withhold forgiveness to FM; I submitted to Holy Spirit's consistent yet gentle and quiet, prompting. I was set free.

Next, I went through many sessions of Inner Healing where I could bare my soul to Christ Jesus and hand over my negative feelings to Him.

Now I am experiencing the reality that although I can still remember the negative events that had happened between FM and myself, my memory is growing fainter and fainter. On top of that, if I do recall the events, I do so with no rage or bitterness. I can now accept that FM did not know what she was doing and that she and I are living in a fallen world.

# CHAPTER 15

# Blessing My Enemies

Matthew 5:44-48 NLT.

"But I say, love your enemies! Pray for those who persecute you! In that way, you will be acting as true children of your Father in heaven. For he gives his sunlight to both the evil and the good, and he sends rain on the just and the unjust. If you love only those who love you, what reward is there for that? Even corrupt tax collectors do that much. If you are kind only to your friends, how are you different from anyone else? Even pagans do that. But you are to be perfect, even as your Father in heaven is perfect."

When my foster mother came to visit us in Singapore, I arranged for two ladies from Kum Yang Methodist church to talk to her about Jesus. The women pointed out my acceptance of Christ, urging her to do the same. My foster mother's response was yet another blow to me. She replied, I did not matter. What mattered was her son (Chinese culture, sons were more important than daughters). My foster mother said that if her son believed than she will follow suit. Her son did accept Christ Jesus out of desperation as he was in financial difficulty. Then true to her thinking, my foster mother accepted Christ Jesus. How gracious is Christ Jesus! He accepts both my foster mother and her son at their point of understanding.

I managed to persuade my foster mother and her son to attend a Brethen church which was walking distance from their house.

At the funeral wake of my foster mother's son, my brother, an elder from the church informed me that prior to the Lord taking my brother home, the elder had the impression from our Lord that he was to visit several church members who did not fully understand that salvation was by Grace, not by works. My brother was one such people. When the elder asked my brother if he was assured of his salvation, my brother replied that he had been doing good works (his daughter informed me that her father's 'good works' was accompanying the church to visit some poor people).

After the elder's explanation both my brother and his wife accepted Christ Jesus by grace. This is yet another merciful act and love of Christ Jesus to my brother and his wife!

Unbeknownst to me, I was blessing my foster mother, her son and her daughter-in -law.

**'5th Commandment** Exodus 20:12 NLT.

*"Honour your father and mother. Then you will live a long, full life in the land the Lord your God is giving you."*

By God's grace I was able to practice the above commandment. I did so by financing my foster mother in the following ways:

1. Finance her cataract operation.

2. Providing her a live-in helper when she had dementia.

3. Buying her disposable adult diapers.

I did the above because I was living in Singapore and my foster mother was living with her son and his family in Kuala Lumpur. Both her son and daughter in law were elderly and unemployed. However, I did not fully realise that I was practising the 5$^{th}$ commandment until my counsellor connected the dots for me.

# Chapter 16

# My Reflection

Philippian 3:12 - 14 NLT.

"I don't mean to say that I have already achieved these things or that I have already reached perfection. But I press on to possess that perfection for which Christ Jesus first possessed me. No, dear brothers and sisters, I have not achieved it, but I focus on this one thing: Forgetting the past and looking forward to what lies ahead, I press on to reach the end of the race and receive the heavenly prize for which God, through Christ Jesus, is calling us."

1 Timothy 6:11-14 NLT.

"But you, *Timothy (Quan), are a man (woman) of God; so run from all these evil things. Pursue righteousness and a godly life, along with faith, love, perseverance, and gentleness. Fight the good fight for the true faith. Hold tightly to the eternal life to which God has called you, which you have declared so well before many witnesses. And I charge you before God, who gives life to all, and before Christ Jesus, who gave a good testimony before Pontius Pilate, that you obey this command without wavering. Then no one can find fault with you from now until our Lord Jesus Christ comes again."*

NB: Words within brackets are mine.

I want to heed, by God's grace, the instructions given by Paul to Timothy because I want to cooperate with the Lord Holy Spirit to fulfil:

Ephesians 3:14 - 19. NLT.

*"When I think of all this, I fall to my knees and pray to the Father, the Creator of everything in heaven and on earth. I pray that from his glorious, unlimited resources he will empower you with inner strength through his Spirit. Then Christ will make his home in your hearts as you trust in him. Your roots will grow down into God's love and keep you strong. And may you have the power to understand, as all God's people should, how wide, how long, how high and how deep his love is. May you experience the love of Christ, though it is too great to understand fully. Then you will be made complete with all the fullness of life and power that comes from God."*

I say a hearty Amen to Ephesians 3: 14- 19.

# PART 3

# My Future: Jesus Redeems

# Chapter 1

## My Name

Philippians 1:6 NLT.

*And I am certain that God, who began the good work within you, will continue his work.*

**Side note:**

Even as I am now, 8 December 2024,
I am crying. I repented
once more to Father God for
embracing that ungodly thought (that I am nobody's child) for
many, many years.
I am glad that as I repented once more

## BEAUTY FROM ASHES

I am being healed of yet another layer
of deep root of rejection within me.
Further healing was granted to me by
my heavenly Father when I attended a
Christian meeting on 6 December 2024,
During the altar call, Pastor/Prophet Alvin, School of Prophets, said
'Heavenly Father wanted to give His
children a hug and invited those who
 needed that hug to go forward to
receive Heavenly Father's hug.'
I ran to the altar. I was second in line.
Pastor Alvin gave me big hug,
something that I did not know that I was yearning for!

Thank you Abba!

# Chapter 2

# More Experiences

Joel 2:25a NTL.

*"The Lord says, "I will give you back what you lost to the swarming locusts, the hopping locusts, the stripping locusts, and the cutting locusts. It was I who sent this great destroying army against you."*

I had been perplexed over the sentence, *'It was I who sent this great destroying army against you,'* for many years.

To me, I often thought:

How can it be that God is the one who sent the destroying army against me?

He is a good God, isn't He? From my reading of articles of mature believers in Christ Jesus I learned that God is Not the author of evil; Satan is.

However, that piece of information did not help me at all.

I thought to myself: If Satan was the author of evil, then why didn't God destroy him right from the moment he rebelled, and save mankind of all the pain and suffering? It was not until after my deliverance on 25 November 2022, that I received revelation from the Lord.

I understood then that the Lord allowed the unhappy relationship with my foster mother to take place because He knows, that in His Kairos moment, He has the power to deliver me. All that had happened to me was for the glory of my Lord Christ Jesus' finished work on the Cross.

My journey with the Lord was also a preparation for my ministry that He has for me. What is my ministry?

## My Vision.

In the 1980's, I had a vision of the Lord handing over to me a child. The Lord carried that child with His outstretched arms. I saw that that child was limp; no life at all. Then I saw a circle of very happy children holding hands and dancing, and the Lord was in the midst of them. I was perplexed. I asked the Lord: 'Why give me

## More Experiences

the limp child when I was a limp child myself. Why not give me the happy children?' The Lord did not answer me then. However, much, much later, after many years of inner healing, the Lord reminded me that I did not receive the limp child. I responded by repenting and accepted the limp child.

From my reading of mature believers in Christ Jesus, I learned that I was a 'wounded' healer. I would be able to empathise and journey with brothers and sisters in Christ, who also had wounded souls better, not perfectly, as I am still a sinner.

# CHAPTER 3

# Return of My Losses

**Lord fulfilling His promise**: Part 1 of this book, page 49: Helen's friend.

**Art .** I attended the following, most of which were subsidised by Government funds of Skill Future Funds and Silver Academy.

> a. **Nagomi Pastel Colours:** This is a Japanese art form that uses soft pastels and fingers to create gentle, soothing, and harmonious pieces. The word 'nagomi' means 'harmony calm, and peace'. Nagomi art is a form of art therapy that can help with relaxation, self-care, and reducing stress and depression. It's suitable for people of all ages and skill levels, and there are no rules or right or wrong. The focus

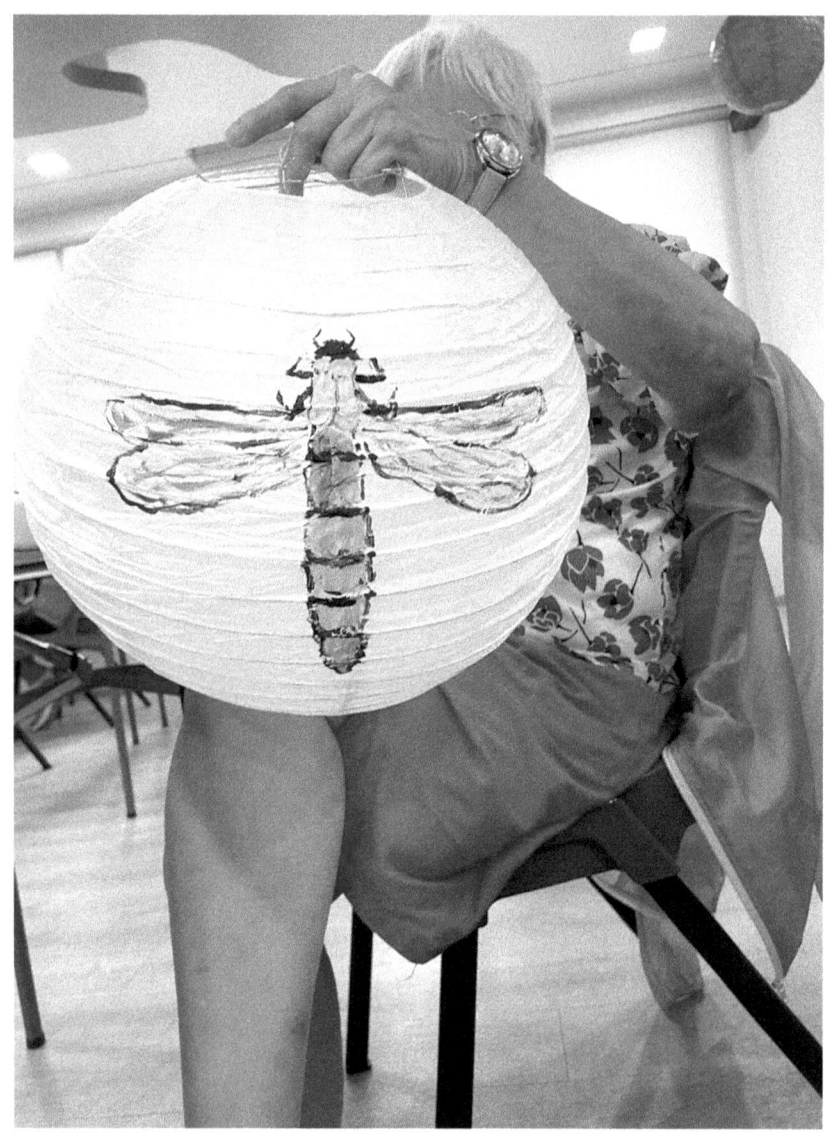

is on the creative process and the calming effect it has on the artist, rather than the finished project.

The art pieces that are in the three parts of my book are samples of Nagomi art.

b. **Sketching**. At this course I learned how to sketch with pencil and also how to use watercolours.

c. **Craft.** I learned this at En Community Services, Pasir Ris West. This is an interest group, so I only have to pay for the materials for a nominal sum of $3.00. Then my hubby and I signed up as volunteers to help participants who signed up for the craft. We are also volunteers to help old folks at Ntuc Care home, Pasir Ris.

d. **Lanterns.** Help Gardens by the Bay and Pasir Ris Elias Community Centre to paint lanterns that were provided for Moon cake festival.

e. **Styrofoam Ball.** Helping Tampines East Community Centre to paint concentric designs on to Styrofoam balls of various sizes for 2024 Ching Gay float.

f.  **Bottle Craft.**

Helping participants who registered for the craft at En Community Services.

g.  **String Art.** Helping Tampines Changkat Community with string art for the installation of the newly renovated community that is due in February 2025. (Insert image 11)

h. Christmas and Chinese New Year crafts

Helping participants who have registered for the projects at En Community Services.

# Return of My Losses

i. **Interest Group.** Learning the ukelele plus singing.

Learning to draft and sew blouse and pants at En Community Services.

j. **Learning Nyonya Cooking** from Pots and Pans, Centre Point, Orchard Road.

k. **Plants** from one day workshop and several days' workshop on hydroponics.

l. **Writing:** I was commissioned by Lord Christ Jesus, when I was set free on 25th November 2022, to write a book that told of my 46 year journey with Him. I asked around for help among my friends, but I did not receive any positive answer to my request. By early 2024, I asked the Lord how was I going to fulfil His commission when I could not find an editor. He replied almost instantly. I came across an Australian company, Ultimate 48 hours Author, on FaceBook. That company has been giving me professional help to write my book.

m. **Music:** I learned to play the ukelele with a subsidy from Silver Academy. By learning the Ukelele I have the joy of joining a jamming session with fellow believers. I could also sing along as I strummed the ukelele. My ukelele 'kakis' (local term for group) had the privilege to bring Christmas joy as we played and sang 'Silver Bells' and 'Jingle Bells' to residents of an old folks' home.

n. **Resumption of our teaching overseas.**

The Lord helped my husband and I to fulfil His commission to me to bring His other sons and daughter back to Him by opening doors for us to minister overseas, mainly to poor pastors.

o. **Teaching**

   i. The Lord led me to attend a one year counselling course at Temasek College which landed me with nine years full time school counsellor post at two schools i.e. Tanjong Katong Girls' and Pasir Ris Crest Secondary.

   ii. The Lord led me to take a course on Montessori Education for children. Next, the Lord led me to 2 ladies who were interested in teaching phonics to children. Together, we shared our resources. From that sharing, the Lord helped me to form a syllabus to teach K1 children (age 5) to be able to read by the end of K2, confident to enter Primary 1. I found that I was in my elements when I taught the children.

It was such a joy to me to see children who had no inkling of phonics graduate from my programme, confidently reading and, speaking clearly, pronouncing the consonants at the end of words. One of my star students was a girl who had short tongue. When she came to me, she had slurred speech. When she graduated from my programme, she was able to speak and read well.

Her father was so appreciative of me that he gave me a big hamper each on Christmas and Chinese New Year.

p. **Restoration of our Marriage**

The differences in the personalities of my husband and I are like that of the differences between day and night. Among our many differences, I would like to cite some:

1. My husband is more outgoing while I prefer to stay home.
2. My husband can find things on his table top among the many piles of items while I like to organise my things.
3. My husband does go to bed between 11pm-12 midnight. I am usually in bed by 10pm.

In the earlier years of our marriage, we could not manage our differences and I asked for a divorce. After some time, my husband also asked for a divorce. A friend tried to help us by sponsoring us to an Enjoying Marriage Weekend, conducted by Ron and Betty Wiseman. We went to that weekend very reluctantly. At that weekend I heard the Lord saying to me:

*"Is anything too difficult for me?"*

The result of that weekend was that both my husband and I went for individual counselling and we slowly worked out our differences. Through the counselling we learned to let our differences complement one another instead of letting our differences divide us.

Praise the Lord that He has restored our marriage. We are enjoying our marriage like never before. On 21st July 2024, we celebrated our 48th wedding anniversary. My husband also joins me in all the activities that I had mentioned above, much to the envy of a lot of wives who attended activities alone.

And last but most important redemption of all, was the Lord's restoring me to my biological family. The Lord did that through my biological mother who gave me 4 'angpow' (red packets with money inside) to my husband and my two children. My 'angpow' had double portion of money.

My elder biological sister passed the 'ang pows' at the funeral wake of my biological mother. In the Chinese culture that incident is very significant, a formal gesture of officially accepting me as a daughter in my biological family.

## Gratefulness

I want to register a Big Thank You to my heavenly Father for letting me discover my skills in art, music, my Interest in cooking, sewing and gardening and, restoring me both spiritually to Him and, here in the now, restoring me to my biological family.

As I reflected further on the return of my losses by my heavenly Father something dawned upon me: I was longing to take part in those activities as far back as when I was in Primary school! Thank you, heavenly Father for Your Faithfulness to return to me my lost opportunities. Last but not least of all, I want to thank Lord Christ Jesus for informing me that He did not make a mistake when He allowed my foster mother to adopt me. He informed me that I was given a good English based education as my foster mother had registered me in both primary and secondary convent schools. He also told me that I was taught obedience through my foster mother, although I did not appreciate it then, for I had to obey in order to survive.

Lord Christ Jesus told me that now I am better able to obey Him and, obeying Him reap His blessings.

Deuteronomy 28:1 NLT

*"If you fully obey the Lord your God and carefully keep his commands that I am giving you today, the Lord your God will set you high above all the nations of the world. You will experience all these blessing if you obey the Lord your*

*God:…"*

I pray that by God's grace, I will increase in my obedience to Him and His Scriptures.

**Hubby is 75 today (2 May)!**

# Part 4
# Conclusion

My life has been a miracle under the loving, gracious hand of my Lord and Saviour Christ Jesus.

Life had given me a bad deal. I had been searching for a sense of identity, belonging and acceptance from my foster family, the Khors. I did not succeed. I only landed myself in cycles of depression. I got out of this rut when I finally accepted the Unconditional Love of my Lord Christ Jesus. After walking with Him for 46 years, I could finally answer 4 important questions. The questions are:

1. Who am I?
2. Why was I born into this world?
3. What am I supposed to do with my life?
4. Where will I go after I die?

My answers to the above questions are:

1. I am the daughter of the Most High God:

    *John 1:12 - 13 New King James.*

    But as many as received Him, to them He gave the right to become children of God, to those who believe in His name: to those who were born , not of blood, nor of the will of the flesh, nor of the will of man, but of God.

    *1John 3:1 New King James.*

    Behold what manner of love the Father has bestowed on us, that we should be called children of God!

2. I was born to have a relationship with the Living, Loving and Merciful God by accepting His free gift of salvation of His Son, Christ Jesus, who came as a man to die for my sins; and is now resurrected and seated at the right hand of my Heavenly Father, always interceding for me.

3. I am to serve my Lord and Saviour, Christ Jesus with all my heart, all my soul and with all my mind, all the days of my existence here on earth.

*Matthew 22: 37 -40 New King James*

Jesus said to him," You shall love the Lord your God with all your heart, with all your soul and with all your mind. This is the first and great commandment. And the second is like it: ' You shall love your neighbour as yourself. On these two commandments hang all the Law and the Prophets.'

4. And last but not least, after I die, I will return. to my Lord Christ Jesus and spend eternity with Him. In heaven I will not experience death, nor sorrow, nor crying. I shall have no more pain, for the former things have passed away.

My Lord Christ Jesus who sits on the throne in heaven shall make all things new, for His words are true and faithful. I will experience the truth that my Lord Christ Jesus is the Alpha and the Omega, the Beginning and the End. I shall experience the fountain of life that my Lord Christ Jesus gives freely to me who thirsts. I am learning to be an overcomer of my circumstances while I am still living here on earth.

I would like to share with you, my readers, a song by Laura Story. This song helps me to continue to trust and obey my Lord Christ Jesus until I see Him face to face and dwell with Him in Heaven.

This song also helps me to understand the Grace of my Lord Christ Jesus, which encourages me to embrace Him even more as my source of strength in my many, many times of need ; be it my emotions, health, finances, relationships etc.
http://youtu.be/sL1DNipyurM?si=vHOvOaE5ifBsxxQa

## Conclusion

Then when I am in heaven with my Lord Christ Jesus, I shall inherit all things and my Lord Christ Jesus shall be my God and I shall be His daughter.

*Rev 21:4-7 New Kings James.*

My most dear readers,
Would you not consider receiving my Lord Christ Jesus as your personal Saviour n Lord too?

# About The Author

Quan Ruby is 75 years old and is married to loyal and devoted husband Ho Hoe Sing.

Together they have a lovely family with a daughter and a son, and two grandchildren. The Ho family represent three generations of believers in Christ Jesus.

Quan Ruby was adopted into a complex family system. As a result of that complexity, she suffered from a loss of identity and low self-esteem. She experienced cyclical depression from the 1960s to the 2000s, with the most severe episode occurring from 2016 to 25 November 2022.

She was set free from her depression by Christ Jesus and is now a very joyful person.

After her deliverance from depression, Quan Ruby received a commission from Christ to write a book to document Christ Jesus's journey with her, how He helped her stage by stage, to be whole again in her spirit, soul and body.

Christ Jesus wanted Quan Ruby's testimony to encourage many, who might have issues that are similar to hers, to give their troubles to Christ Jesus so that they could also be set free from their past and have a secure future with Christ Jesus.

# Notes

# Notes

# Notes

NOTES

www.ingramcontent.com/pod-product-compliance
Lightning Source LLC
Chambersburg PA
CBHW040108100526
44584CB00029BA/3907